This book is dedicated to all the brave people
on the front lines fighting this virus and working hard
to provide care and comfort to those who need it.

Christmas is coming, but it's different this year.
Will it still be merry and full of holiday cheer?

The pandemic has changed things, we know this is true
But the spirit of Christmas will always shine through.

You can still share Christmas love and make someone's day bright,
Try baking cookies or going caroling at night.

Everyone loves getting a card in the mail
Or buy the perfect present when you find it on sale.

Your grandpa, your grandma and other family,
may be celebrating Christmas virtually.

Even though you may be miles apart,
You know they are with you, inside your heart.

Kissing under the mistletoe?
During a pandemic, the answer is no!

Try a nod, a bow or tapping your feet.
Blowing air kisses would also be sweet!

Will Santa still deliver presents this year?
Will he still give gifts to kids far and near?
Santa's a hero- he's up for the task!
He'll deliver the presents while wearing his mask!

Santa's elves are social distancing with six feet of space.
They are wearing their masks to cover their face.

Even Corona can't slow down these elves!
They are working so hard to fill the toy shelves.

Milk, cookies and hand sanitizer
are the perfect things to leave out for Santa's appetizer.
He'll be pretty hungry and he'll need his hands clean
Lots of houses and germs, if you know what I mean.

Reindeer can't get sick, so that's a relief.
They will fly all night for Santa their chief.

Santa will get to everyone on his list
If you have been good, you will not be missed.

This year you might find that it is better
to write Santa Claus a Christmas letter

Its better than meeting him in a crowded place.
You can make your requests but still keep your space!

Get out the frostings and the cookie baking pans,
But first please make sure you wash your hands!

Kill all the germs by using lots of soap
Preventing the spread of this virus gives us all hope.

If canceled Christmas parties have you feeling sad,
there is still plenty of holiday fun to be had.
Go for a drive to see Christmas lights,
shining bright and giving hope on dark winter nights.

Or get beautiful ornaments and decorate your tree,
filling your family with happiness and glee.

Are you going to a place that might be jam packed?
Remember to where a mask and avoid close contact!

Decorate your mask to show some Christmas cheer.
Try Jingle bells, bows or a red-nosed reindeer.
Even though its covered up, don't forget your smile.
A big Christmas grin is always in style!

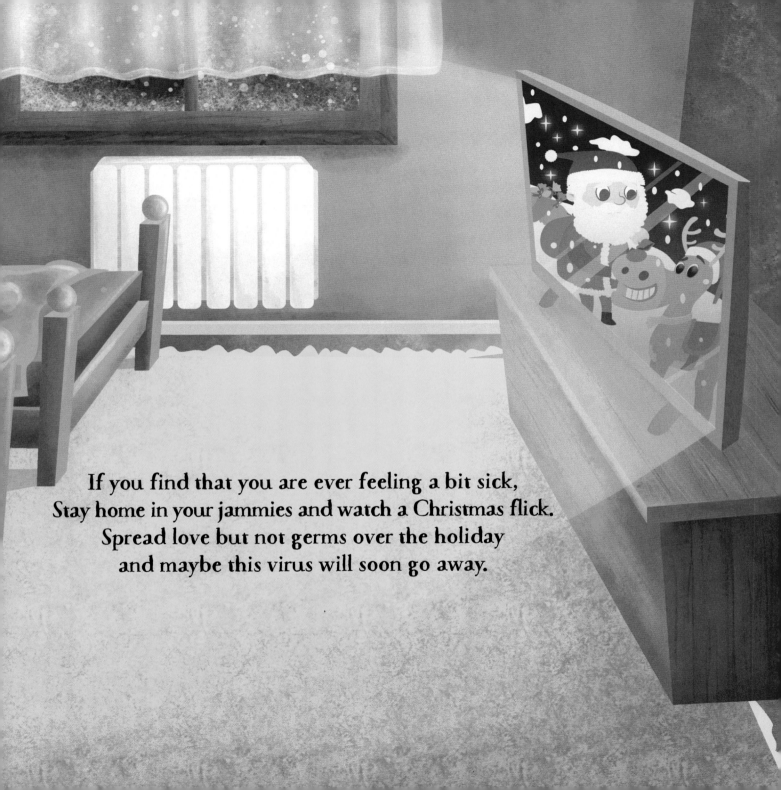

If you find that you are ever feeling a bit sick,
Stay home in your jammies and watch a Christmas flick.
Spread love but not germs over the holiday
and maybe this virus will soon go away.

Doctors, nurses, those on the front lines,
Delivery drivers that have tight deadlines,
Sales clerks working to stock the store shelves.
These workers are giving so much of themselves.

So be sure to give them a smile or wave
To show you appreciate them being so brave.
The virus has made their work harder to do.
Take time to give them a big thank you!

The Christmas season should be
filled with joy and delight,
It's a time to show love
and do what is right.

Keeping the world healthy is more important than ever
Remember this in every holiday endeavor.

You can be a kid-hero and make the season bright
Christmas and kids can help the world unite

Putting others first is the most important way
you can make sure everyone has a happy holiday!

Merry Christmas!